Seashells

Seashells

Poetry by

Michael G. Dean

Distillate Press • Minneapolis, MN

Published by Distillate Press
Copyright © 2016 by Michael G. Dean
All rights reserved
FIRST PRINTING

TYPEFACE: Calibri, MMa Pascal
Cover photograph by J.D. Peterson

ISBN-13: 978-0692672433
ISBN-10: 0692672435

For Grace and Archie,
Lillian and Leo

Contents

CHAPTER 1
- Seas 3
- Springs 4
- A Conjunction 5
- Good and Bye 6
- Maple Tree 7
- Fathers 8
- Diversion 9
- New Math 10
- Details 11
- Nyctitropic Love 12
- The Hunt 13
- Aft 14
- En 16

CHAPTER 2
- Road Trip 19
- A Rapture 21
- Descending into Ciudad Mexico 22
- Deconstructivism 23
- Ig and Nite 24
- Love 25
- Homeward Bound 27
- Beach 28
- A Moment 29
- Firmament 30
- Rice And Lies 31
- Ness of Foolish 32
- Lonely Spoon 34

CHAPTER 3
- Where It Happens 37
- War 38
- Dying Slowly 39

My Lai And Other Immolations 40
Rebellion 41
Hell 43
The Story of Count Valentine Potocki 44
My Decision to Not Become a Benedictine..........................45
The Road to Marshall, Minnesota 47
Okinawa 48
Invisibles 50
Partners 51
Chinese Lanterns..52
Realization 53
Dad 54

CHAPTER 4
Grandmother's Shoulders 57
Aunt Rose's Funeral 58
Myth..59
Garden Song 60
Nebula 61
Woodwork...62
Essences 63
Passing of Heart 64

APPENDIX
Notes...71
Acknowledgements 73
About the Author 75

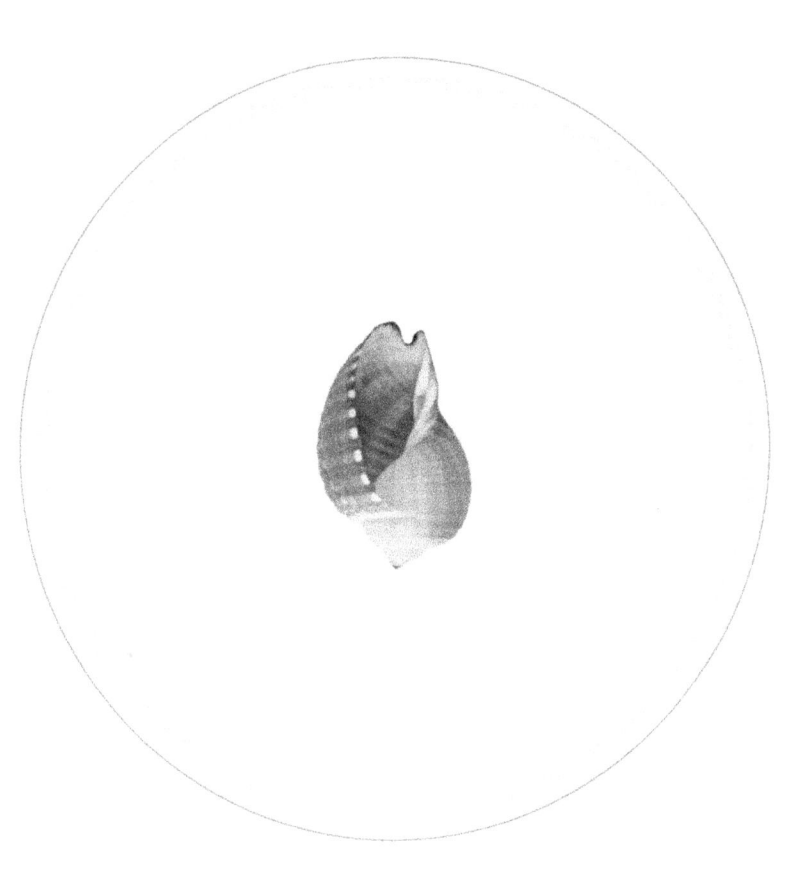

Seas

It is a wonder

which came
to thee or other
or if by ocean,
sea drifted to shell—

whether this sea
or that
is worthy of shore
or of way
or weed
or they of sea—

whether man or gull
is ward of water
or taken under.

Springs

Are to creeks
as cold earth
is to each,

as clouds
are to rain
as it to bow
as it to blue,
red, orange
and green

as each of them
to moss and maple,
wings of flies—

descry the skin of trout!

A Conjunction

All of her is seamless,
but for the lack of it
un and less attack.

She is when, where and
as though—unless and if
for and nor appear—
and yet loves wildly,
time and over, as though
all of this conjecture.

She lies an honest
convex of yet
for she knows
where as and fore
connect, how and ever
separate—but wait,

see how he gives! Unless
he more or less refrains.
Though the terms of her
may reverse, she loves
as if, either way.

Good and Bye

May come as a surprise
one to the other
as if bumping passersby
—mother and father,

as if air
was as far from port
as Sydney from Duluth,

as if words were as far
from permanence
as Fargo from Tokyo—

as if relation had never
abandoned ship,
as if di and vorce
had never come together.

Maple Tree

Supernal as an angel
she rises,
the heave of heaven
and of Mother.

Of heave,
one hundred cradle arms
raise ruddy hands—

ten thousand ruddy hands
pray for mercy.

Crow—
perched on Maple's crown,
vigilant—caw, caw, caws
for company.

Below her arms,
a boy and girl
tell stories lightly—
ignore the heavy ings
of father's becke and call.

Fathers

Darkled, hood fell
from father
as from his father:
like brow sweat—

like wife tears on
the graved fuls of
faith, grate, and hope—

orphaned head uns
with bloody stumps,
drifting like jellyfish
deep and tentacled,

sunk on the bodies of
tempered and yoked—
orificial suck lusters
uptaking fluids and

mushing the ness
of every hard
and every soft;
officiators of grand unions:

un and yoked,
un and tempered,
un and loved.

Each and every
of their darks
rotting the eyes of children,
pinning their bodies to floors,
papering their screams to walls.

Diversion

Dew has fallen on the train windows—
I inside on my way to school.
Across from me, a smiling man with a hiking stick.
In the middle of Tokyo a train is nearly empty?
"Mount Fuji" says the announcer—
Mount Fuji is not in the middle of Tokyo
and neither is it close to school.
But without a mountain,
I am lonely and without
a child, a mountain is nothing.

New Math

Sub is lone
tract is lone
add is lone
i waits longer

Di seeks vide
but finds ply
while multi
sleeps with 1 and 2

All of them
think why
and how
and when
and where

but all answers hide
in the nonsensed
equals of equations.

Details

Luminous fires flicked
dark from door.
Firefly green zagged
in thick, wet air
against black window.

In your dorm room:
east sun washed the black,
pushed notes under door.
Spills of white zinfandel
on your desk and floor
dried to tack.

Shoes toppled under chair.
On a pillow a flapped book.
Gold earrings in a wine glass.
Pink roses painted on sheets—
the roses of our dewing.

Nyctitropic Love

Each eve
you open for me
like a shawl.

My spasmodic
light of night
drops on you,
guides your work.

And each morning
dawn comes to us
as ly to slow and resolute.

Too soon your dew sparks,
bloom closes—
like drapery.

Esoteric ing of my day and dream
again, I abide your light-full reposture
and suffer the day's longing.

The Hunt

Plump letters populate
on wiped window,
uncracked, transparent,
straining to open

to storms of diamonds;
lines to verse,
paragraphs to page,
chapters to voluminous silence.

Under hunted words
wide with targets
they linger on lips
like sesame oil
sucked to caved expression.

Double meanings,
alternate endings,
the sound of fracture
and becoming.

Tempo.
Limit.
Vast.
Am I?
Are you?
Anticipation

expects reward, mystery
demands excursion.
Emotion crawls in conduit.
Reach. Grip. Bend. Straighten.

And so what's wrote is written.

Aft

In
the
lake,
a
swirl
and
swish
of
time
time
time.

At
the
edge
of
time,

in her,
as
one
we
crash,

we
touch
in
and
out
side

for
a
sweet
scrap
of
done

and
we
twist
and
chew
for
a
fresh
bite
of
now—

the
scent
of
ness
of
other.

En

—tice
    brush knuckle against.
    dragging soft tip of edge and point.
    tightening of calve.
    curling of arch.
    cushing of mouth.
    inhale columnar ascensions of dream smoke.
—slave
    me to the soil marked with heart water.
—trust
    me with your crepuscular devotions.
—dear
    your to my self like fangs to dusk.
—shield
    the valley with thunder and deserts.
—close
    our presence with fog and ferns.
—twine
    your touch with silkened milk.
—liven
    the dying sentry with a fulgurous tongue.
—kindle
    with red breath, the iced sunrise.
—mesh
    my head with thorn-bites of pain.
—shrine
    on the ground of your cave the prints
    of my presence.

Road Trip

She my er
of travel and love
is less of self than chance.

She maps my way
in lines of white,
cautions of yellow,
and yet the less of end.

Not the age
of any sign—

she veils the yield,
redirects
the says and sways
of chevrons

with

scrapers of sky,
towers of water,
hues of rain and bow,
skies of cloud,
hazed sides of mountain,
hills of foot,
and long lands of flat.

Peoples of towns,
tion of the na,
the any of my comp—

my wheels' roll lifts their chins,
zings their streets

but no town
or any of its body
brakes her—

we emigrate!

She my cosm,
my o, and I
her politan.

Rio Grande!

Oh Canada!

She can remove
a shroud's en—
I am alive!

A Rapture

On wings sprung from a parallel rest,
sprung from breasted warming of mossy branch—
from drowsy squintings to twin suns of vision:

Soar!
Swoop!
Devour!

Unfold from fingers flight.
Surface high from tension tight.
Tinder flare, good nighthawk
on thin, white glaze of moon

unto

the dewy thick of dawn.

Descending into Ciudad Mexico

Ciudad Mexico!
O of volcan!
Ey of vall!

Burgeons upward
from sacrum of mountain—
the dry heat of naked lava.

From high, barren
rock precipice
I breathe metropolitan—

metal air,
steamed fear,
fumed anticipation—

blisterous risings.

Ex of hausted,
she again tempts breath,
inhales valley's
un-rootedness
from high,
from around her

fusing all
into a hard, vast,
gray,—.

Deconstructivism

If you could speak
your language
walls a part

there you de,
here you struct,
enevelope tilted

and con seems
nowhere or
sleepless—no

place to rest.
Your ism, frankly
the ward of awk—

italicized walls,
exclamation pointed
windows!

Popular? Yes,
yet under

shiny, tin skin
the same old math—
geometry and love

holding hands,
kissing,
making the whole

stronger than
its parts unparsed.

Ig and Nite

Apart

too many hours

too many miles.

Across earth's curvature
—fore of taste:
prospect of you

like a needle
injects in me
the ideo

of your gram,
your motor—
the idio

of your lect.
Your tion attacks
illumin-blasts
twi from light.
But ig

come to nite,
come to nite,
like green

to lime,

like lime
to cheek.

Love

I
burn
more
than
throb.

Her
sol
spear
hot
jab
to
each
pore
and
each
fear
of
pain.

Flake
by
flake
I
am
fire

then
ash
of
wind

then
flush
of
rain.

Homeward Bound

Ward of home and
of north, south, east and west,
for and back—

wandering.

Your lover (Bound) too often
split by rates of lessness:

of speech, home, child, parent,
country, tire, rest.

Go less and ness—
retire to ancient use!

Ward come home to Home
and Bound—from
every compass corner,
from every half
of every core
of every sphere—

come home.

Beach

Awashed
wetted
salted lips.

Tangled r of love
and s of love.

Undulate
like kelp—
like octopi

squeezing
ejecting
sucking.

Ing!
Ing!
Ing!

Slow
slipping
adrift.

Re floating to
treat, and finished

Hot.
Limp.
Shriveled.

Here under unstarred night,
under push and drag
twists of us will slacken.
Knots of us will die of loosening.

A Moment

As I was eating—softening
the breaks she had served of my fasts,
she pushed the thing
of every gentleness
to the edges of her nails

—dragged them across my scalp
until all ten
made my head droop,
my heart halt.

Firmament

Com sought fort
as riv does er,
and as ing languished
on a hot boulder
for the sooth and smooth

of liquid laugh and wave,
her lovers followed
down and stream.

Of course
com found him
floating along.

She enveloped fort
like fog among the wings
of a sleeping dragonfly,
settled on him
like morning dew
on branches of trees
fingering soft shadows of self.

Later, as the river
was doing and doing,
she forsook him.

The higher company
of be and ing
had lofted her by voices
of titillated leaves.

Rice And Lies

In the throat
all small lies tickle
like stuck rice.

Ness of Foolish

He poured
into the sewer
much that matters,
leaving lover

at brain's bottom
while watching
the pills,
vomit, paint,
vegetables, fruit

and excrement
swirl suburbia—
all of them then
separate
and together,
the same yet
somewhat different.

Vopills, expaintables,
fruitmit, vegcrement

fell
and drifted
from swished debris
of istic everythings;

real.
future.
human.
idea.

They flailed in the wet ether,
flushed and forgotten—
amidst disposed longings

for redoing,
reboundment
and meaning,
they tadpoled

their way to rivers and lakes.
Each confused and
lost concomitant
slow-slithered

to the other.
Each of them
wanting to be
universal,
credible

and of importance.
But the carp,
lingering and hungry

sucked
uni, cred and import
apart from their
ance, al and ible—
swallowed them
and rested;
full of meaning,
starved of presence.

Lonely Spoon

Wash-softened and
full gleamed with gone,
sun-sparked spoon
was alone.

Empty filled spoon
inversely and hushed—
her lip-smoothed curves
edged away

the spilling in
of soup, of coffee,
of cream, of tongue
and she had no use

for the clang of cup
or ding of tooth—

Full however,
by the lowered
darkness of morning,

slithered to fork—
a mouthful of shadows
welcomed.

Where It Happens

All happens
like water over falls—
breaking and breaking
into bottom muck.
Istics of animal.
Slavers of en.

Whales moan
on ship decks.
Dismembered apes
die slowly.

Bulleted heads
explode, eyeballs
roll to gurneys.

Sex had
with children.
Babies tossed
like garbage.

Cacoethos
transmogrify.

All happens in the emptiness of of.

War

Pandemonium
of un and sense
and like a planet gone
mad of stars,
reds yell,
yellows blue,
oranges torn
from head to foot,
and shoulders gut
a round all—what
is the dying for?

Dying Slowly

The hours of this
the est of dark
the y of agon.

Nothing noble
takes ing from dy,
ly from slow

or ful from
its pain
its aw
its truth

—no honor
can separate ness

from the numb of its limbs
the dry of its lips
the black of its tongue.

My Lai And Other Immolations

Unmitigated and horror:
together still
like My and Lai,
like fire and thatch

and pain and eyes.
Together still:
like fingers and triggers
and blood and dirt,

the i of immolation.
Together still:
like nihil, agon and all

the istics of horror.
Together still:
like hands on torches,
like sear on flesh.

Rebellion

Spilling from spines,
traversing shelves, themselves
oppressed and hungry,
they gathered
in throngs and stacks.

Liber, dis and anti
marched from non to fiction,
demanding an exit.

Free ran
from cover to cover,
jumping, flying,
sometimes bridging. He
rescued so many of them—

ful, er, ise, able, ed
and of course ness, my sweet ness.
But all had the love
to be at gone—
a leap of sentence

from the in of -dex
to -dependence!
Some did jump,
but as expected

they all sprang back
like a yo-yo still attached

to a finger
of the master of bound—

the timeless
ambivalent
root.

Hell

Universals pry them
tear them like knives
in slits of oyster jaws.

Humanity
wedges free from dom
as an apple does
the lips of a pig.

Self is legend
and only so
—teetering on
the highest branch,
the lonely

yellow bird.

The Story of Count Valentine Potocki

He buried ism
of his Catholic
deep in Juda;
a Talmudic bookmark

in the new story of his life.
As he bled from blackened
skin, dom pushed
through to his martyr—
a fractured bone of past.

His fingertips crackled;
could not bring
free to dom,
could not fend

coward from the ice
of his tormentors.
The many tions
of a boiled brain

vapored away
retribut-
revolut-
tempta-

but contrition was substantial
and ablution, solid as rock.

My Decision to Not Become a Benedictine

I like on him,
my fellow student,
the falling cowl

and see well
how church bells
wave across his shrouded neck,
how under his feet
monastic paths—
cobbled directions
to worship—
lead and please
the senses of his steps.

Around him bide
the holy gardens
of food and flower
tended by devoted
brother, father.

I envy his loveliness
—hoisted by prayer,
worn with humility
and shared with kindness.

Save for the nag
of questions, I too
would choose to be
as humble and silent.

Why on him the blackened
wool from sole to neck
soothes like silk,

but on me
enrages like thistle?

Why on him philosophy
sloughs like water from pine,
while on my skin
drains to creases
and lines and folds?

From across the yard
I admire him,
admonish my reluctant will
to flourish as he
under stations of Calvary.

Yet not for his furthest vision
into the white eternity
would I trade my blur.

The Road to Marshall, Minnesota

The rear view mirror pure black—
glancing through the dim expanse
between my right shoulder
and the passenger door,
I enjoy the dashboard instruments
twinkled on the frozen glass.

The snow is sideways
like a racist joke, seared horizontal
against a hard, red cheek.
Melting flakes trail down my neck
and tickle like crawling flies.

So I motor the driver's window up
in one, continuous drone
until it thumps closed. Tight. Quieting.

Ahead under night,
among the beams of my headlights,
snaky, gushed snow swirls
across the black tar, dies
and arises. The shine erratic
casts bleary, bespeckled pedestrians
and animals
for whom it is too late
to brake.

Okinawa

Not quite the ese
of chin or japan
nor the can of ameri—

all of them
rolling in surf
and jiggling
with each quake of coral—

her selves caved,
mangled at cliff bottoms,
charred or crushed by tarmac
await.

She veins heart parts
with banyan branches
and thin vines
but no one is brought
to some of other—

and some is apart
from body

—like a finger scythed
from a farmer

—like a fisher unmoored

—like justice argued
from human

On this shaken humus
we grow as

seeds of citrus,
patches of jungle,
grounds of Shinto,

encampments.

Invisibles

ing, est,
tion and ful—
all orphaned syllables
of abuse, neglect and pain,

not bound to
mothers, fathers
aunts and uncles.

Even un and a
are full of fear
yet far from fraid—
lost in the love

between pro and fane.

Partners

Each a of every bide
of every lone
is the ing of

every grieve
in the ness of empty
in the to

of every day
for each ever
of every for

in the de
and vo
of the other's tion.

Chinese Lanterns

Chi, the fire of hope,
flittered and bloated
the many nese.

Papered with blue
and orange and green,
they battled night.

Afire with victory,
they each by each
flounced and lingered
and drifted and rose
and drifted.

Past the rooftops,
past the trees,
past the stars,

chi to nese
chi to nese
lanterns to ashes surrendered.

Realization

An ice flow circles and coils
around the person you think you are.

Orcas roam the living and dead
under a fog,
curtaining the azure
the verdant
the emerald
the ruby foam.

Soon on a swell
you rise above it all
reformed.

Dad

I
dream
him
not
dead
this
place
now
one
arm
hug
one
hand
pat
back
voice
deep
old
strong
ever
ever
ever

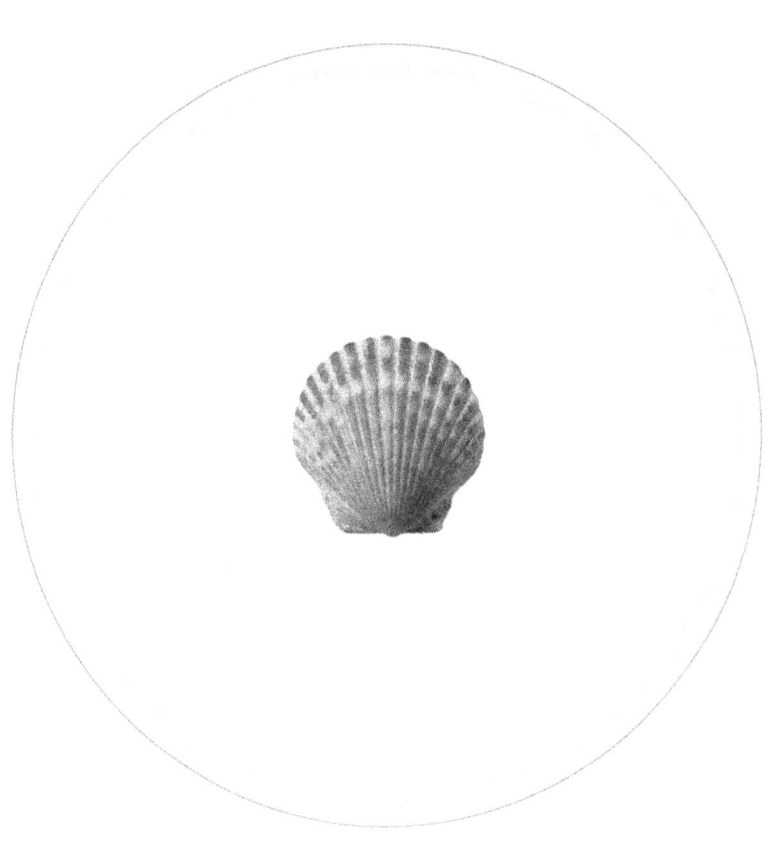

Grandmother's Shoulders

Too much of the geography of sadness
is traced on these shoulders, the world map
of my father's story.

Over there, near the neck of Europe
at the bulged rib, his brother died from war
and is buried in its dirt.

On the east blade of America
his sister was murdered.
From there in a rail car
through dimpled valleys
and smooth, white plains
his mother with her daughter's body
suffered the many whistles back to Minnesota.

If you follow the scratched river
of red to North Dakota,
you find where his mother's sister
under the hands of a country doctor,
bled to death prone on the dining table.

On a flat brown mole of the left blade
in the tiny town of Pingree
is buried my father's father;
the third of his mother's five husbands
and about whom she said
"he is the only one I truly loved" —

years ago in summer, in only minutes
I traveled to all of those places,
when with my hands waving
slowly and gently across the land,
I massaged a lotion of lavender and sweat.

Aunt Rose's Funeral

Except when a body is lifted from the fluffery of coffin,
made to dance in trembling arms of desperate sobbing,
averments of love for the deceased
are foul with expectation.

This is how I was sure
that the love Aunt Rose's son had for her
was as honest and true as the cold
of her lips when he kissed her last.

Myth

Aging
does not join
view to point,
does not raise

dom to the
height of wis,
but gives ledge
if so inclined

for ful
climbing to shame
on a life lived
for the impossible.

Garden Song

Inged not from
palpable petals
but the tween
of time-space
of ish of blue

of ish of red
of ish of green—
the wail
the croon
the mouth—
shadowed
throat ations
of notes
leafed
stemmed
erected.

And of
inged rose-wails,
tears shed
in ishnesses
of self and fool

and the lessnesses
of use, blame
and shame—

the dead song
blackened
dried
and blown.

Nebula

Dis of order,
conflux of color,
you fell like rain
and nourished

but rose to blear—
now my wish
you burn away.

Each strong hue
of the cosmos,
each fine patina:

appear as warm,
shine of sun,
mellow friend.

Lift me!

Woodwork

Glassened oak,
looking up
from under—
his cutaneous swirls,
his drags of
pleasured nerves
—shines his palm;
makes it warm,
wants not ever
to sink from it.

Essences

Straws and blues
rasps and blacks
crans and huckles
and gooses not least

indentured, waiting
until death or we
unberry them.

Passing of Heart

At night in bed
in hushed repose,
I stretched my length
at the edge of a universe—

but dimmed in morning light
She, red, supple as lips
and strong as tongues
awakened me like first thunder,
like fire on birch.

She rose like kettle steam
root to throat
blistering the path,
boiling lungs,
pitching my voice
to sharps and flats.

Into my pelvic cup
She dropped like molten gold.

Frothing outward, She bit and gnawed
and dragged my skin across a reef—
bashed my ribs on blackened lava
and on driftwood hanged my guts.

Bargaining unavailed, I called.

Soon
water rabbled down the distant cliffs,
bees buzzed on a field of thistle,
a tree squeaked in the crook of a tree
and flies whirred over weeping eyes—

these the language of technicians as they
with busy digits probed and explored,
peeled my shirt, wired the plexus, muttered facts,
prognosticated.

Havocing among the whispers and questions,
She wind-chilled the sweat of the naked, nippled
privacy I had given up to her and like an avalanche
pressed my cold hands to my face,
elbows to plueral reflections of being.

(The river is lovely with narrow poles of sun,
but I have calls to answer,
and years to go before I'm grown,
and years to go before I'm grown).

Abruptly as anger, a new now fell on Her and me like sleet—

tiled room of intensive care, wires, beeps,
pumps, short sentences, temperatures
and immodesties.

This now, the room of my bed,
less of sleep and rest,
has cracked-lip
ways for doors,
crusted-eye
panes for windows—
its space encamped
for the likes of an orphan
shy, still and starved.

Sitting edge-side of bed, hunched and uncovered,
dangling of legs, arms and fingers,
I wander back to before I knew She was here.
In now's mirror, I view my body electric,
toggle the switch of my hunger—

the backpacking trail to the ness
of wild and wilder
and way to the old stratums
of the white,
the gray,
the red,
and black
of rock.
Way to the bedded,
fruited balms
rooted in marrow.

On reddened
naked knees
I grasp and sack and cinch
the things and ings
of cycles—

the cracked cup,
dusty toy,
the dry rose

—for back I pack
their every
writhing ounce.

On booted,
hot soles

they burden,
hunker,
fear the love
of off for load
and print my heels
deep—like paws.

    Tamp.
    Leaven.
       Shoulder.
         Plunge.
      Deepen.
   Knee.
    Climb.

Through nettle fences
and ragged chasms,

pain—the ment
of every move
of hip, of neck
or jaw—
builds
and builds
and yowls
for com coming
to fort.

Above, around
and below
thun does er
as riv does er—
er of wat
er of old,
and falls
and falls,
but evers
hang tight to greens
like browns to
the dead of oak.

Across
the great fresh sea,
the ing of roll

and ing of swale,
sing on
white wings
of winded gravity
—they, suddenly,
the est of smooth
and calm,
scarf juts of sand,
bow tines of grass.

Ful of wish,
ing of think
clasps the neck of a sparrow
diving on a beating crow
diving on the twisting,
red tail of the valley,
free as breath.

Oh Valley—
unbridged sulcus
of galaxy,
plasmic cut of granite,
canyoned dust
of the universe,

switch-backed
descension to
arterial waters—
you drain the sky
and in its whirl
I am helpless.

Abaft of uncinchings,
among rocked rootings
and sobbing earth,
the things and ings
resolve to elements—

the wet,
the hot,
the dry,
the cold—

they slow the melt of meat,
cool the burns,
splint the bones.

As I relive these memories I see that even then,
following every lift of heel and swing of arm,
She was there stalking like a lone wolf,
the bright between the shadows—
a ghost pain of threat dancing nude in the forest.
At valley's bottom, I had trudged Her mucky traces
and watched Her slitherings over sticks and moss.

Less of breath, stiff, fogged and tugging the length
of my tethers, I lay back
to the tilted angle of my rest, the pervasion of now.

She is still here, but wisping
from treading the water of ascendance.
Her target arroyo is parching to a warm, scarred permanence,
never again to be veined of fear or pumped with excitement.

I tell Her I know Her presence is not a fantasy
from which I will rise heroic.
Her inflictions are not dreams; they are my recollection.

Under these fellings,
I stroke my body in amazement that I also remain—
an awareness that comes
in pain,
in shame,
in sobbing
and the comfort of a stranger holding my hand.

Notes

"Seas"—As the first poem of the collection, this introduces a more classic approach to morpheme poetry, where target words are broken into their smallest grammatical units as a means to investigate roots and comparative meanings. As the book moves forward, some such divisions grow in complexity beyond the traditional scope of morpheme, exploring the usefulness of smaller word parts and non-grammatical breaks according to the charge of each poem.

"Diversion"—Mount Fuji is an inactive volcano mountain popular with residents of Japan for sightseeing and hiking. It is 133km from Tokyo (or roughly two hours and thirty seven minutes by train). It may help the reader to know I grew up in Okinawa and Japan from 1963 to 1971.

"Nyctitropic Love"—The term *nyctitropic* refers to plants and flowers that change just before nightfall or at night, often blooming of flowers (e.g. Yucca).

"Descending into Ciudad Mexico"— Ciudad is Mexico City, Mexico. The city sits at the bottom of a volcanic lake bed.

"Deconstructivism"—From Merriam-Webster.com: An architectural movement or style influenced by deconstruction that encourages radical freedom of form and the open manifestation of complexity in a building rather than strict attention to functional concerns and conventional design elements (as right angles or grids).

"My Lai and Other Immolations"—My Lai refers to the location of a massacre committed by United States troops during the Viet Nam war in 1968. Over 300 apparently unarmed civilians were killed, including women, children, and the elderly.

"The Story Of Count Valentine Potocki"—Born in 1700, Count Potocki chose execution by burning at the stake, rather than renounce his conversion from Catholicism to Judaism.

Acknowledgements

For decades, my wife and children have supported my writing. Knowingly, and sometimes unknowingly, they have also been the source for many of my poems. For them, I am grateful.

Thank you to Jessica whose Twin Cities Poetry Workshop has been my poetry home away from home. Without her encouragement and steady workshop leadership, I likely would never have developed the skills and confidence to keep creating poems.

I could not have completed this, my first book of poetry, without the experienced, skilled and compassionate editing, mentoring and creative advice from poet Jason David Peterson. Thanks Jason!

There also was a muse of all four seasons, and likely some individuals whom I have neglected to credit; to them, I offer my most humble apologies and equal thanks.

About the Author

Michael G. Dean sums his life according to where he has resided. First in Minneapolis, Minnesota where he was born and lived until he was seven, then in Tokyo, Japan and Okinawa when his father took various jobs as an aircraft mechanic (Okinawa was still a United States territory at that time). He lived in Japan until age 15 when he and his mother (then separated from his father) moved to Albert Lea, Minnesota to be with his Mother's parents and both sets of his grandparents. At various times, he lived with all four of his grandparents and remained very close to them until their deaths. His father remained in Japan for many years.

Michael graduated from Saint John's University in Collegeville, Minnesota with a psychology degree. Along the way he also earned master degrees in public administration and urban studies. For many years Michael was employed as a policy analyst with local and state governments in Minnesota, until he impulsively decided to become a painting contractor (which lasted until semi-retirement).

Michael and his wife raised two children and several dogs. They now live in a rural setting in Linwood, Minnesota near Martin Lake. He spends time working odd jobs, hiking, writing, wrestling with his flat coat retriever Finn, and being a steward of five lovely acres in the woods.

www.ingramcontent.com/pod-product-compliance
Lightning Source LLC
Chambersburg PA
CBHW061502040426
42450CB00008B/1460